Published with ♥ in Fall 2020

To Mom, my co-editor.

To Fran, for the bracelet.

To Bil, for loving me because *and* despite.

Why Chin Up?

Is there something you tell yourself when you need a boost? For me, it's "chin up." This is what I whisper to myself when I feel embarrassed or afraid, when I am uncertain, when I need to get to work, when I remind myself in the swirl of the day the kind of person I want to be.

On August 19, 2019, I started a personal project to tweet a daily message of encouragement. And I chose Chin Up as the refrain because it is so often what I need to hear.

"Make a tiny offering," I said on December 24. That's what this morning tweet was: a tiny, regular offering to my friends and colleagues and strangers and the world at large. Sometimes silly, sometimes sappy, sometimes heavy, sometimes half-formed...and almost always an attempt to send light into a world that held a lot of shadows.

And also it was a gift to myself. Some days the message flowed forth, and other days I ground out some combination of words that didn't say much of anything. By doing it daily, for one year, it became a practice. I respected (and also resented, some days) the discipline of it.

And what a year it has been! I turned 40. I left my job of 13 years, one of the great loves of my life. My husband and I gave up on fertility treatments; we grieved and began to accept a new and unexpected version of our future. God willing, we experienced the final year of the presidency of Donald Trump. Oh, and we entered a global pandemic that turned every aspect of our lives upside down.

Personally and collectively, it has been a year of vulnerability, change, questions. Of paradox: isolation and community, uncertainty and clarity, fear and resolve. On my best days, my Chin Up practice gave me a way to make sense in real time of what I saw and felt—and a chance to articulate my confusion on the rest of the days.

What I didn't anticipate, but came to rely upon, was the company. Chin Up became a source of connection. What a lovely thing it is to realize that when we reach out, the world responds richly and warmly. I've been rewarded with cheerleaders, friends, and co-authors. I have seen how people can understand the same words in very different ways. I received inquiries as to my well-being, laughs, new correspondents, and exuberant greetings from strangers. The reactions were sometimes a great surprise and often a delight.

Almost a year in, I took a look back at these Chin Up tweets and was somewhat surprised that most of them held up. Taken together, they even start to form a loose kind of philosophy.

The themes are not hard to find, and they're not particularly novel. Be kind. Try hard. Say the scary things. Love your people. Love your place. Love is an active thing, it is so much bigger than any one person, and it is up only to you. And, mostly, the philosophy is *the practice*. Notice things. Share what seems important. Learn in public. Put yourself out there.

So that's what this is. A tiny offering, with my gratitude for being part of my year, part of my journey, part of me.

And always, always: Chin up.

Monday, you snuck up on me. Chin up.

Tuesdays can be rough. They lack the newness of Mondays and the progress of Wednesdays. Chin up.

> Sometimes showing up (interpret that as you wish) is so much harder than I expect it to be. Sometimes it turns out to be the easiest part. Here I am anyway, Wednesday. Chin up.
>
> *August 21, 2019*

For us anticipation addicts, Thursday is the most beautiful day of them all. Chin up!

Angsting about the impending end of the weekend, month, summer, year? Me too, but maybe we can put that on hold in honor of Friday. Chin up.

Saturday is for sunshine, possibilities, doughnuts, late starts, car shows, daydreams, campfires, and romance novels. Stretch it out. Linger. It'll end, but we can pretend it won't. Chin up.

Holding on by my fingernails to Sunday. That's all. Chin up.

Just for today, I will try on curiosity. Ask more questions. Ask better questions. Wonder why instead of what now. More "hmm"s, less "okay, so"s. It's only one day; what could happen? Chin up.

Just for today, I will suspend my disbelief. Anything is possible. All intentions are good. The world is a soft cushion. There's room for third chances. Believing makes it so, right? Chin up.

Just for today, I will be mindful of who and what I let in. Good energy only, please. Leave the snark at the door. Kindness is the price of admission. (Treats are nice, too.) Shields up, chin up.

Just for today, I'm going to give myself a reprieve for mistakes I've made, typos in my tweets, stupid things I've said, perfect things I didn't say, 7th grade bangs, other lapses in judgment, and toothpaste on my shirt. Lay down the things you carry with me? Chin up.

Just for today, I will dream out loud. Let's whisper-shout all our hopes into the universe, just to see who's listening. Chin up.

Just for today, I'm going to be selective about what I get worked up about. Maybe this is another way of saying: rest. Chin up...

Just for today, I will sing as if it isn't September, I weren't tone deaf, I was singing backup to Bruce Springsteen, I didn't have neighbors. Belt it out like we mean it. Chin up!

Life lesson: Transitions can be hard. New beginnings are precious, though, even when driven by the calendar. Get ready to jump, people. Hold my hand? Chin up.

Life lesson: Tuesday after Labor Day is the 8th longest day of the year (after the first week of March which is the 8th circle of hell). The rest of the year starts now. No way out but through. Chin up.

> Life lesson: People have reasons. We're all dealing with complexity. All the times I've assumed and been wrong, all the times I've prejudged and been humbled. Ask why x100, and accept that other people's reasons aren't mine to know. Chin up.
>
> *September 4, 2019*

Life lesson: morning always comes. Chin up.

Life lesson: When someone reveals a piece of themselves, it is a gift. It's on me to hold it with care and wonder. Connections, big and small, shrink this scary world to a manageable size. Chin up.

Life lesson: Sometimes tweaking around the edges will get us where we need to be. Sometimes we need to burn it all down. I try to choose my strategies carefully, unless they choose me first. Chin up.

Life lesson: Show up. (Related: it's okay to leave early.) Chin up.

Mondays are for solidarity. We're going to get through it together. Activate the buddy system...now. Ready? Chin up.

Tuesdays are for character. We're in it now; no going back. Helmets on, strap in, barrel through. We'll be stronger, wiser, tougher, more human on the other end of today. Chin up.

Wednesdays are a bridge. It can be long, the lanes might feel a little narrow, and sometimes there's a toll, but we end in a different place than we started. And, if you can take your eyes off what's right in front of you, the view! See you on the other side. Chin up.

> Thursdays are for wishing. All of the possibilities *just* around the corner. Let's not waste our wishes on small things. Chin up!
>
> *September 12, 2019*

Friday, our reward for participating. Even if you aren't sure you deserve it, take a victory lap. Chin up.

Saturday, and I'm under the dryer at the hair salon. Chin up.

I have learned to reject absolute statements. I've crossed too many lines that I drew in sand that shifted under my feet. Absolutes are crutches. Let's leave room for context and have faith that we will know what's right. Chin up.

Someday, I will sing in a gospel choir. Maybe just one song, in the back, without a microphone. Maybe as backup to Bruce Springsteen on the steps of the Lincoln Memorial. You never know. I'll be ready. Chin up.

September 17, 2019

When I'm not ready, do not underestimate my ability to avoid, ignore, press pause, equivocate, reframe the question, tap dance, make tangential lists, color code my files, or write briefing memos. It's part of my process, and we catch up with each other eventually. Chin up.

"Let go." I must've heard this a dozen times yesterday. Knowing when to step aside, and how to do it graciously, might be the hardest human thing. Sometimes holding on is persistence, and sometimes it's stubbornness. Chin up.

Good morning, eastern time. I've missed you. Chin up!

Some days, we do the things we thought we couldn't do. Chin up.

Today, we celebrate the 70th birthday of Bruce Springsteen, who taught me that it's okay to let them see you sweat. In the words of Bruce's mighty mom, "lace up your dancing shoes, and get to work." In other words: chin up.

The day might hold things we're not looking forward to, like, say, the dentist. Maybe it will also bring an unexpected block of free time, a song we haven't heard in awhile, and surprise treats! Who knows what can happen. Chin up.

Did you know that it's Thinking of You Week? Handwritten notes are the embodiment of my top two rules: If you have something kind to say/do, don't wait. And: Words matter. To all the letter writers and time takers, thinking of you. Chin up.

I have finally learned how to send text messages with balloons and confetti, so pretty sure it's going to be an amazing day. Chin up! 🎈 🎉

Timing. The inescapable factor that makes life so challenging to plan forward. The universe moves at its own pace, for its own reasons, not to be understood by me. Chin up, be ready.

Long week? Here, too. Making a pile in the corner of the unfortunates, unnecessaries, and oopses that I don't need to carry into next week. Rest up, chin up.

To all the people who get your clothes ready the night before, is this the secret to life? Tell me how you do it. Chin up.

> The people who make you believe you can do the thing you didn't know you wanted to do, who make you laugh at yourself in the middle of a rough day, who light up your insides? Wrap them up tight. They're magic. Chin up.
>
> *October 1, 2019*

Patience.
Patience.
Patience.
Chin up.

October 3, 52 degrees, sunset 6:23 p.m. Wearing a jacket, squirreling away acorns, taking some outdoor breaths before they hurt. Chin up.

Waiting on a sunny day. (Don't @ me, Bruce fans.) Chin up.

I've been in New Jersey for 18 hours and have met two people with real-life-Bruce-encounter stories. Keep your eyes open, people, and chins up.

Good morning, early risers and snooze-button pushers, poets and candlestick makers, Monday lovers and more-of-a-Thursday types, master chefs and takeout purveyors, diehards and temperature takers, secret holders and those who say it all out loud! Chin up.

Good morning, music makers, map makers, sense makers, bread bakers, place makers, memory makers, mood makers, model makers, chance takers, history makers, and (most importantly) day makers! Chin up.

Good morning, litter collectors, local buyers, voters, fence painters, community gardeners, Little Free Librarians, sidewalk sweepers, door holders, flower basket artists, and neighborhood fish fry ticket holders! You make the world better. Chin up.

Good morning, people who have no idea where their umbrellas are. Chin up.

Good morning, history enthusiasts, introverts, park lovers, secret romance novel readers, tramps like us, slow runners, people who are happy listening to sad songs, list makers, and those who appreciate a good morning affirmation. You are my people! Chin up.

Good morning to the people who say the things I need to hear (even if I really don't want to hear them). Keep nudging at me. Chin up.

Good morning to the people who stand along the route with cheers and high fives. Your cowbell keeps me moving! Chin up.

Good morning, people who make fancy hearts and dog faces in my hot chocolate. What's better than making people smile? Chin up.

> Good morning to everyone working their butts off for a dream. We've got this. Good morning to those who are trying to figure out what the dream is. We'll get there. And good morning to everyone just getting through. There are times when that is the noblest thing. Chin up.

Good morning, to those who back into parking spaces slooooowly despite a line of cars behind you. I'm sure you have your reasons. Chin up.

Good morning.
Take the chance.
Take the time.
The consequences.
The lead. The fall.
Take the stage.
The stairs.
The long way home.
The bait. The cake!
Take the first step.
The next step.
The last munchkin.
Take what you need (no more)
today. Chin up.

October 17, 2019

Now give it all back. Chin up.

Good morning to everyone using their Saturday to do something big and important. It's worth it. Chin up.

Good morning and happy coffee making to everyone who tried to get @JohnMarionjr to try a new coffee maker. Chin up!

Good morning to everyone whose first instinct is to say heck yes, of course I will, I love you and here's why, it's going to be okay, I'll bring snacks, thank you and here's why, don't read the comments. You are the companions I choose for the day. Chin up.

Good morning! Today, throw a lifeline, a party, a message in a bottle, a Hail Mary, a tantrum, a curveball, a bone. Throw away that which doesn't serve you, throw some stuff against the wall, throw some feelers out. Whatever it is, put some muscle into it. Chin up.

Good morning. Sometimes I think I am too [ ]. But maybe the world needs more [ ]. Maybe someone I meet today is longing for [ ]. Maybe I was put here, right now, to bring the [ ]. So I say, let's see whatever [ ] you've got today, people. I'm here for it. Chin up.

Good morning, sunshine. Today is all about soft landings. May you enjoy them, may you offer them. Chin up.

October 25, 2019

Good morning to all those who hold strong opinions on celebrity weddings, commas, thank you notes, proper funding for libraries, the necessary time to arrive at the airport, and turtlenecks. For maybe 6 things in life, we're allowed to think we're absolutely right. Chin up.

Good morning to every person who has had to sit in their car and breathe for a few minutes before getting out to face the people and the day. Go easy on us, Monday. Chin up.

Good morning to everyone who woke up feeling unreasonable. The light is changing and so are we. Push hard, stretch it out. Make the world hear our expectations, even if it has no intention of remembering them, even if we plan to change them tomorrow. Chin up.

Good morning, fellow travelers. Today, there is work to do. Hurt to soothe. Problems to solve. Holes to fill. There are burdens to carry. Trees to plant. Races to run. Wounds to tend. But first, always, we check in on each other. You good? Chin up.

Good morning, people who know how to wear scarves. Good morning to all the rest of us, too. Chin up.

Good morning. Today, may we write like @mkimarnold, smile like @Deb_Baum, serve like @RamonaESantos05, sass like @fntpvd, lead like @meganranney, organize like @PatCrowley401, run like @FitzProv, paint like @JordanSeaberry, and rock like @springsteen. Chin up.

Good morning, Saturday. Hooray for rest stops! Stretch your legs, use the facilities, stock up on snacks, consult the map. Watch all the traffic speed by from a safe distance. Chin up.

Good morning. Sunset is at 4:37 p.m. today, so soak in the ☀! Chin up.

Good morning. There is going to come a point today where things feel really dark. Luckily, we have a few hours to prepare. Stock up on snacks and smiles from strangers, activate the buddy system, and remember: today is not the day to question our life choices. Chin up.

Yesterday wasn't my
best day. Today, though!
Today has promise.
Isn't this the way?:
We stumble, we rise;
we speak carelessly,
we apologize; we tire,
we rest, we try again.
Again! Chin up.

November 5, 2019

Good morning to the above-and-beyonders. You know them; they're the people who say nice things when they don't need to, strive for extra special when good enough would be fine, take the time to say a very specific thank you. There are heroes among us, if only we notice. Chin up.

Good morning, restless souls. Feeling the urge to both run away and dig in? Yeah. There is something out there for us. I feel it in my chest. Maybe you see it around the edges of your vision. If we're going to break things today, let's do it for the right reasons. Chin up.

Good morning, friends. So what shall we do with this day? Chin up.

Good morning. Sometimes I forget but you remind me: There is beauty all around us. There is strength deep within us. There is grace between us. Notice these things, seek them, spread them. Chin up.

Good morning, New Englanders. It's time to turn the heat on. Chin up.

Let's do things that matter. Chin up.

Good morning. Snow in the forecast, Tuesday that's a Monday, the overlap of road construction and holiday planning seasons, and Mercury in retrograde. It's understandable if we're a little off today, is what I'm saying. No sudden moves. Chin up.

Good morning to everyone who expected of the world something a little different than the world expected of us. Oh, perhaps that's all of us? Chin up.

Good morning. On any given day, we are all a little weird, all a little sad. A little uncertain, a little scared, a little lonely, a little awkward. It's okay; we have each other for company. Chin up.

Good morning! May today's sunshine warm all your cold spots. Chin up.

Good morning! Are you exuberant about your loves? You are my favorites. I don't care if it's stamps, Springsteen, sci-fi, tripledeckers, or snacks; whatever you care about, let's see it. Let's hear it. Don't shortchange the world your enthusiasm. Chin up.

Good morning. Sundays are for dreaming. Dream big. Dream broad. Dream deep, wild, bold. Dream in words and feelings. Dream in poetry and bullet points, formulas and music. Dream heroic and heartbreaking. Dream in promises you make to yourself and those you scream aloud. Chin up.

Good morning. My 69.75-year-old mom is taking ice skating lessons. So I think you and I can take on this day. Chin up.

There are days we can alter the direction of the universe, and there are days to accept what comes. Days to question everything, and days to do the work before us. Days to say what needs to be said, and days to prioritize kindness. Good morning; what is today? Chin up.

Good morning. When we're doing something that matters to us, it doesn't need to be graceful. If it isn't easy, we don't need to pretend it is. Awkwardness is frequently a consequence of doing something important. Chin up.

Good morning. It's a brand new day. Break it wide open. Tear through the wrapping. Bounce it against the wall. Dance with what the day brings us. Throw it up in the air to see how it lands. Climb atop something and proclaim the wonder that will be this day. Go at it. Chin up.

Good morning. Words! Words can make our hearts swell, race, sing, skip, ache. Choose carefully, use generously. You all have outdone yourself with the words this week. More poetry to accompany us through today, please. Chin up.

Good morning to everyone who has mastered the critical life skills—like passing on the second cookie, remembering names, keeping your humor when you need to reset your password yet again, maintaining an adult-like inventory of toothpaste. The rest of us, keep striving. Chin up.

Good morning. Somewhere, the sun is shining. Not here, not today, not yet. But we'll be ready. In the meantime: I'll be self-soothing with sweatpants and hot chocolate and waiting for this damp, drizzly November in my soul to pass. Chin up.

Good morning! 2020 is impatiently creeping closer. December is crunch time for resolutions. I'm hereby convening a support group for those of us who fell a bit behind this year. It's time to take on that thing. (Yeah, that one.) (I know.) We believe. Chin up.

Good morning to those who are generous in your endorsements, compliments, connections, likes, recognitions, and thank yous. Life is a lot, so let's not hoard appreciation. Chin up.

Good morning. Here's to those who hang in there for uncomfortable conversations when it'd be easier to withdraw. The words may not come perfectly, the feelings may be messy, but presence is a really good place to start. Bravery in relationship is its own special kind. Chin up.

Good morning, Thanksgiving. Giving thanks, starting with you. I am grateful for your companionship, for the things you teach me, for the ways you make our world better. Chin up.

Good morning. Today is a day for sorting. This I can control; this I can't. I will hold on here; I will let go there. These things are worth the time, the calories, the investment, the consequences; these things aren't. May we make good choices. Chin up.

Good morning. It is said, when one door closes, another opens. It's tricky business, though. It might take a long time and a lot of work to find the second door. It might not even look like a door. There are thresholds to cross, all around us. Step with purpose. Chin up.

Good morning. December! A month of contradictions: Beginnings, winter is upon us; endings, the last days of the year. Cold weather; warm sentiments. Darkness, shortest days; light, twinkling everywhere. What will the month bring? Chin up.

Good morning. For today, a reminder that there are lots of ways to show up. Mine might be a little different than yours. Today might be a little different than tomorrow. What matters is that we're here. (You're with me, right?) Chin up.

(Love in my family looks like a 5:50 am text from my dad to be careful in the snow. Is it the warmest feeling to wake up and discover that someone has already been thinking of you?) Good morning, friends. It's messy out there today. Take good care. Chin up.

Good morning. Now that we're through with the traditional post-Thanksgiving days, we get to come up with our own themes. I'm declaring today Persisting Wednesday. One. Inch (step/meeting/minute/mountain/breath). At. A. Time. Chin up.

Good morning. Apparently, it's time for all of the *people of the year* lists. I nominate you. Yes, you. Prepare your acceptance remarks. Chin up.

Good morning. Resolution season is my favorite. The possibilities! Who's got big/tiny, exciting/important, wholesale/incremental plans? 2020 me can't wait to meet 2020 you. Chin up.

Good morning. Stay warm today. Bundle up all the important parts: limbs, extremities, head, heart, secret thoughts, all the feelings. Chin up.

Good morning. The end of the year is when list makers shine. Here were the year's victories. Here are the people we lost. Those who deserve holiday cards. Things I'm going to do next year. It feels like sense-making to sort things into neat piles, however temporarily. Chin up.

Good morning. Some days, we've just got to do the thing. It's okay to vent or grumble. Say a few bad words if necessary. It's okay to feel sorry for ourselves. For a few minutes. It's okay to have an extra treat. We don't judge what it takes to get us through. Chin up.

Good morning. It occurs to me: The people who stand by us when things go sideways are often not the people we expect. I've come to love the way life can give us exactly who we didn't know we needed. And then everything is different. (And then we are different.) Chin up.

> Good morning. The universe gives, and the universe takes away. The particulars are not ours to control. Is there anything to do but love and let ourselves be loved, whoever/whatever/however, without reservation? Chin up.
>
> *December 11, 2019*

Some days, I don't have much to say. Just: Hi. I'm here. Chin up.

Good morning. There is nothing better than witnessing someone's joyful surprise. If I were in charge, at the end of this precious life, we'd ride out on a slideshow of faces we have lit up. (Doesn't take much. Intention is all. Effort is everything.) Chin up.

Good morning to those people who have holiday-scented soap by your sinks. Not going to lie: you set a high bar. To the rest of us, who buy soap-scented soap in bulk size, there are lots of ways to celebrate. (We keep the scent in our hearts.) Chin up.

Good morning! I'm trying to hang on to the twinkly lights, the warm cider, the greeting cards and communal singing of strange songs and ugly sweaters, the annual presence of Mariah Carey. It's a lot, but we will need some tidings of cheer come January. Chin up.

Good morning. Yesterday, I was reminded how glorious a quiet, dark place for a few still moments can be. If you need to pull the covers over your head for extra minutes today, I'll watch the door. Come out when you're ready. Chin up.

Good morning. Somedays I tell myself, don't break anything today. Today is not one of those days. Chin up.

Well, today's morning tweet was thwarted by an unexpected eye injury. Regularly scheduled programming back tomorrow... (Chin up.)

Good morning. GOOD GOD, HOW IS IT ONLY THURSDAY? Oops, that just leaked out. Roll onward, 2019. March forward, friends. Chin up.

Good morning! The universe has: A wicked sense of humor. A roundabout way of making its point. A lingering case of the blues. A wide view. A lot of time on its hands. The right to change its mind. Is it any wonder we sometimes feel a bit wobbly? Chin up.

Good morning, shortest day. Shine, glow, glimmer, burn, sparkle, smolder. There are many ways to send light into the world. Also, there is magic in the dark. Chin up.

Good morning. Hide your cookies, hide your treats. Save me from myself. Chin up.

Good morning. Yesterday a dear friend asked me, "how is your heart?" I thought about that question for hours. I considered, I concluded, I revisited. Genuine inquiries are a gift (and a nudge). So today I ask you: how is your heart? (You can respond silently.) Chin up.

Good morning. Make a tiny offering today. I will, too. Chin up.

December 24, 2019

Joy to the world. Peace to the world. Dog kisses, baby smiles, chocolate covered oreos. Courage to change. Comfort of a best friend. Curiosity. A cushion of goodwill. Grace for what is and what's to come, grace for others. Light for the way. To the world. To you. Chin up. ♥

Good morning. Many days, it's a slog, but every once in awhile, we wake up to surprise waffles. Life! Chin up.

What gets you up in the morning? (More of that, please.) Chin up.

Love is a verb (the fiercest of verbs). Love is a contact sport. Love is a practice. Love is soft and hard, strong wind and warm sunshine, comfort and itch. Love is ours to give and ours to receive, and sometimes those don't line up perfectly but we try anyway. Chin up, my loves.

Good morning to everyone trying to keep it all together as 2019 rolls (over us) to the finish line. A new year is just ahead. Chin up.

Today I remembered that transitions aren't easy. Sometimes it's too much to think about a whole year coming to an end, another stretching ahead. So I'm going to focus on just this one day. Maybe this one hour. For the next 60 seconds, I resolve to be patient with myself. Chin up.

2019 in review: What're you most proud of? When was your most joyful moment? What was the most hard-won lesson? Who're your favorite people? What's exciting you right now? These are the things I'm taking into the new year. (The rest we can leave here.) Chin up.

Good morning, 2020. What shall we do with you? Chin up.

Good morning. I'm not sure what day/year/decade it is, but did you see the sky this morning? It's going to be a good one. Rise and shine, friends. Chin up.

Good morning. I'm suggesting the first rule of 2020: no regrets for 2019. Nowhere to go but forward. Chin up.

Good morning. If you were going to invite 10 people for a conversation about [topic you care about], who would they be? Maybe, just maybe, the time for that invitation is now. (P.S. I'm available.) Chin up.

Good morning. 2020 is asking a lot of us, so when we can, let's give something beautiful to the world. Light a candle. Light ten candles. Dance. Be silent. Whisper the questions in our hearts. Read our favorite poems out loud. Say all the kind things. Again. Again. Chin up.

Good morning. The first full week of the year is upon us, and with it the real winter season. Testing time for many of us. Nowhere to go but right on through. Chin up.

Good morning. I propose a new rule: we can each only say "you look tired" to two people in our lifetimes. Choose carefully. Chin up.

Today, let's take heart from the people around us. In the face of uncertainty, we can notice, connect, hold, sustain each other. We must! Chin up.

Weeks like this, I forget all about resolutions, good intentions, or even basic manners. *deep breath* Good morning. How are you? I'm here, and you're here, and it's Thursday, the most optimistic of days. So, chin up.

Change is going to come. I can brace myself with anger, stubborn resistance, self-righteousness, the false security of certainty; these cover fear nicely for a time. Instead, I tell myself, be brave. Greet it with curiosity, let it wash over me, become something new. Chin up.

Good morning. Just for today, let's not think too much. All the thoughts will be there tomorrow, waiting for us to think them. Today, we give ourselves a tiny reprieve, a bit of distance, a glimpse of vastness. Chin up.

Yesterday, I visited my mom and dad and was greeted by a cardinal outside the window. Anyway, it has me thinking about signs. Signs from the universe. Signs of the times. Directional signs. Astrological signs. Signs of affection. Warning signs. Ah, but what do they mean? Chin up.

It seems to me that "I've got your back" is the highest expression of commitment. To offer without qualification, to accept without shame. No small things! Knowing soul-deep that we do not walk alone is just on the other side. Chin up.

Good morning. Let's spend a few minutes first thing picking up some of the pieces of ourselves that may have scattered. Tidy up before company gets here. Chin up.

Good morning. I was recently advised, you've got to walk the mile. Lots of ways to interpret that, and I'm pretty sure they're all worthy. March onward, fellow travelers. Chin up.

Good morning. We don't always know what will cause wounds, do we. I suppose we can either swaddle ourselves in bubble wrap or be a little more careful with one another. Two reasonable options; I won't judge which you choose today. Chin up.

January 16, 2020

This week, I was reminded: Leap. Leap! Chin up.

> Good morning. The thing about embarrassing ourselves is that the next day still comes, and we must face the world again. On those days, chin up.

Good morning! The cold, wet, wintry snow makes the sunshine seem brighter, no? Chin up.

Giants have walked among us. They have inspired us, challenged us, called us to higher and better. They are among us still. Chin up.

Good morning. I've been thinking: There is a season for everything. There may or may not be a reason for everything. There are things worth believing even when we doubt them, things worth doubting even when we believe them. In other words, it won't make sense. Chin up, anyway.

Good morning. Let us be astounded by ourselves. Fall in love with the people around us. Commit whole hearts to the places we inhabit. Sing out loud the things we whisper to ourselves. There is no room for half measures on this cold midlife January day. Chin up.

When it comes to enthusiasm, manners, rest, courage, vegetables, and a friend's faith in you, a little goes a long way. (Imagine what a lot could do.) Chin up.

January 23, 2020

Thus far, I've proceeded with the assumption that—at some point— I would know what I'm doing. I'm beginning to suspect that it doesn't work that way. (That changes everything.) Chin up.

Good morning. The marvel of Saturday is that we can fill in the blank. Today, I will be [...]. I will do [...]. I will feel [...]! Early weekend, you make all things seem possible. Chin up.

There are things that get better with age. Important things like self acceptance, perspective, and ability to manage my hair. Notably, memory, digestion, patience, and physical coordination do not seem to improve. (There's still time.) Chin up.

"Everything in moderation," my mom has told me approximately 1,675,701 times. I have more of an indulge-until-you-feel-ill philosophy. It really just depends on what you're aiming for (and what you're willing to put up with). Chin up.

January 27, 2020

Good morning. Shall we squeeze the stuffing out of this Tuesday? Chin up.

May your Wednesday contain unlimited smiles from strangers, your favorite song on repeat, the perfect (for you) amount of human interaction, an unexpected challenge to keep it interesting, surprise free time, at least one victory over your to do list, and good snacks. Chin up.

Let it go, I told myself, but then I considered my other options. Let it out. Let it roll. Let it shine. Let it be. Let it fly. Let it in. Let it bleed. Let it ride. Let it happen. A little bit of each is okay, too. Chin up.

Is now the time to complicate life? Is now the time to say the thing? To learn how to dance? To renovate the bathroom? Is now the time to take a break? Jump with both feet? There are no right answers. Chin up.

Good morning, February. A whole new month! A chance to turn the page, press restart, move on, write a new chapter, shake things up, turn the corner, burn the ships, wipe the slate clean, turn over a new leaf. Unless things were going well, in which case, KEEP ON. Chin up.

Life has a way of reminding me
to love my people hard, however
imperfect or inept or vulnerable
I feel in doing so. Chin up.

February 2, 2020

First Mondays of the month call for something special. Like a 30-minute delayed start, opening song, wear-your-pajamas-to-work theme, marching band performance, recitation of your favorite poem, or 3 pm cookie break. (Every day is a good day for a cookie break.) Chin up.

A wise and brave soul who
knows about this kind of thing
advised me yesterday,
"acknowledge your kickassery."
All day, I whispered that to
myself. Today, I shout it out to
you. Chin up!

Good morning, Wednesday. Sprint, march, stagger, skip, crawl, shuffle, leap, strut, tiptoe, stride, stumble, parade, sashay, limp, scramble, stroll, saunter. Whatever it looks like, however it feels, keep going. Chin up.

Let's set this Thursday on 🔥. Burn, baby, burn. Chin up.

Okay, so we're going on day 38 of 2020 and day 3(ish) of dreary. I know we all have been carrying the orange blossoms in our hearts, but I think it's time to pull them out. Chin up.

Time is uncertain. There's no room for small smiles or half gestures. Do it big. Chin up.

It is chocolate-covered Oreo week! (Every year, my mom makes chocolate-covered Oreos for Valentine's Day. I am not ashamed to say that this has gotten me through some dark winter days.) My point is tradition. And Oreos. And coping rituals. Also, moms. Chin up.

It's Monday, again. So I suggest all of us find one person who is doing something hard and important and brave, who might feel the tiniest bit lonely or strained, and appoint ourselves their personal support crew. Chin up.

> Can't say it any better than Matt did here. Warm the world! Chin up.
>> MATTHEW BILLINGS (@nativevtr): Chase, pursue, get after it hard. Grind until it gives. Warm the world with the fire in your belly.

"Let's change the world," a friend said to me yesterday. These are the kind of co-conspirators and comrades we all need. Grab your people, and let's change the world. Chin up.

"I'm going to see it through," said a favorite older gentleman when I asked how his winter was going. And so we shall—this day, this story, this task, this question, this place, this life. Chin up.

> I'm a thief in the house of love and I can't be trusted." Aren't we all? Take ♥, my loves, and give it. Chin up.

Life philosophy: Pick a few things to care about, and then care like hell. Care wholeheartedly, blatantly, embarrassingly, greedily, fullthroatedly. Plunge into the dark deep end of our cares like the imperfect beings we are. Save our composure for the rest. Chin up.

February 15, 2020

On three, let's all close our eyes and send good vibes across the universe to someone specific for something specific. (Bonus points if you tell them.) Chin up.

One of my favorite meeting practices is "needs and offers." I think we should bring it into our daily lives. I need to stop waking up at 3 a.m. I need to eat more vegetables. I can offer this tweet, a Springsteen song, my certain affection, and a chocolate covered Oreo. Chin up.

Sure, long weekends are nice, but now there's nothing to do but look Tuesday in the eye and say, in whatever tone of voice best signals your intentions, "I'm going to take you." Chin up.

Every once in awhile someone reminds me of the complexity of things, and I am humbled. There is always more. And! And we cannot allow ourselves to be paralyzed. There are only choices and chances, and navigating through this messy life, the best we can, each moment. Chin up.

Is that sunshine? It's sunshine, right? I think so. Let's say yes. The sun is shining on us this Thursday, friends! Chin up.

Today, let us each leave in our wake (in the words of Dale Carnegie) "a friendly trail of little sparks of gratitude." May my trail and your trail cross paths and light up this world. Chin up.

Saturday mornings are our reward for Tuesdays. Stretch it out. Chin up.

Reminder to myself: Don't minimize anyone's sense of loss or source of joy. Honor the feelings. Honor the battles. Chin up.

Words like warm sunshine. Words like the song of your heartbeat. Words like a hug with the perfect amount of squeeze. Words like twinkly lights in a dark room. Words like the first morning stretch. A prayer, a challenge, an offer, a wish. Say them all today. Chin up.

Yes, the hotel provides the magnifying mirror, but we don't need to use it. For today, let's resist the urge to unnecessarily magnify and obsess over and poke at our faults. (Best to keep self-reflection to real size. Proportionality!) Chin up.

One of the wonders of the world is the way people can surprise us. Those known and unknown to us, in ways big and small, lovely and sad. For one quick minute, give the surprise it's due. Absorb the delight, acknowledge the blow, reorient. Chin up.

Vacation, they say. Relax, they tell me. "This is not going to be your typical nice boat ride. This is going to be a very stressful 2.5 hour ride out and 2.5 hour ride back. This is not going to be a pleasant trip." If there is ever a day for this: Chin up.

A thought for Friday: Not everything need be A Great Challenge. It's okay to take the easy way some days, on some things. Chin up.

I should probably say something about leaping today. But this February 29 is more about endurance. An extra day in February when some of us feel like the usual number is more than enough, thank you. So leap if you'd like, go for extra if you can, endure no matter what. Chin up.

> Dear friends, March is upon us. With it: the beginning of spring, more daylight, cookie exchange, and who knows what else. Forward, always forward. Chin up.
>
> *March 1, 2020*

It doesn't make much sense but sometimes I have to remind myself to take the kindness offered. Take the words, take the gestures. We are all worthy of kindness, all capable of it. Chin up.

Put on your working clothes. Square your shoulders. Lace up your shoes. Buckle your seatbelt. Straighten your spine. Secure your mask. Gather your people. Say what needs to be said. Breathe deep. Look today straight in the eye. Chin up. And let's go.

Let's hear it for the wallflowers. Look to the edges of the circle. Chin up.

Do you have a person who stretches for the exact words worthy of this moment? (This is the kind of superpower I'm interested in.) Stay close (they're magnetic). Let the words sink to your toes, let the bravery fill your chest. Chin up.

Blessed are the noticers, sharers, truthtellers, buttkickers, offerers, plan B co-conspirators, reach-outers, load carriers, treat bearers, lamplighters, notewriters, and healers. Those who help us along our way. Chin up.

Gratitude to those who stay in their seats until every performer is off the stage. Honor the work. Chin up.

Today, during this longer day, sit in a patch of sunlight for as long as it will have you. Let it warm you from the inside out and fill the dark, hidden spaces. Know there is more ahead. And when that moment has passed, get out there and light it up. Chin up.

Who will surprise us today, and who will we surprise? What will we give to this day, and what will we take from it? How much will today change us? How much will we, today, change the wide world? Chin up.

When you have someone who believes in you, the horizon opens, the sun shines, the world sings, strangers dance, and the air whispers sweet nothings to you. (Or maybe it just feels that way.) (Which is really what matters.) Find that person. Be that person. Chin up.

> Life seems to have a way of circling me back to places I've been before. This could be my poor sense of direction, but at times it feels more like... closure or karma or a not-so-subtle reminder that I'm not done yet. Here we go, again. Chin up.

Sometimes the shortest distances take the longest to travel. I mean that literally and metaphorically. Pack a lunch. Chin up.

This week has been overwhelming, no? And yet also I marvel at the people glowing through the darkness, holding us up. Let's make some good offers for this day and the days ahead. To start: I'm sending you light, love, and strength. Patience. Courage. Health. Chin up.

Whatever tools you have—words aloud or written, the ability to create beauty, really good hugs, a special casserole, extra toilet paper, generous tipping, spiky humor, exceptional list-making skills, music, a few empty hours—bring them out today. We need them all. Chin up.

Today seems like a good day to suspend our expectations. The loads we carry are heavy; lay down what you can, for however long you can. Chin up.

Uncertainty is the hardest thing. (Inaction is up there on my list, too.) I am reminding myself to look to the things I know to be truer than true. (Your list might look different than mine, but perhaps the principle applies?) Take good care, friends. Chin up.

Being kind in a crisis is one good thing. Sustaining, deepening the kindness, stretching it out over an unknown period of time and happenings, is another. We have a long road ahead. It will look different for each of us. We're going to have our moments. When possible: Chin up.

What's keeping you going right now? For me, it's the funny, generous, confused, honest, occasionally slightly desperate messages from humans across all of my circles. Check in on your people, is what I'm suggesting (especially, you know, if I'm one of your people). Chin up.

A few days in, and some of us are feeling hollowed, brittle, frayed. (Maybe just me?) I can see now that this is going to be a long, treacherous march. We came out strong with positivity, support, and snacks. Now we have to settle in, pace ourselves. For the long haul: chin up.

Today I woke up angry. While it doesn't feel good, angry feels better than confused (and confused feels better than sad, and sad feels better than lost). In other words, I have a long way to go. But somewhere in that messy pile is acceptance and agency. I believe. Chin up.

For those of us hanging on by our fingernails, barely putting on pants, uncertain how we'll manage what's to come: Just hold on. Just hoooooooold on. Just. Hold. On. Chin up.

> Let's remember: we vote with our feet, our dollars, our voice. This is a washing away moment. We are no longer beholden to the way things have been. To get the world we want, we have to put our backs into it. With every choice, we can care for the people who care for us. Chin up.

March 22, 2020

Good morning. Things are blooming outside. Open the window and say hello, sing a line, recite a poem, ask a question. Say what you've been meaning to say. The trees are listening. Chin up.

Eight days in, I can say with confidence: The hardest thing about social distancing is my inability to get away from myself. Nevertheless... Chin up.

Wednesday. News is grim, getting grimmer. From what I can see on here, a lot of you are having to learn fractions. We're out of the emergency snacks. But in the words of the heroic @meganranney, "we have to be in it, to get through it." Chin up.

What I'm telling myself today: It will not always be like this. I will not always feel the way I do now. Look forward, look forward. Also, the usual: Chin up.

Note to self, there's no shame in:
    "Forgetting" to turn on the video.
    Crying.
    Spending a few extra minutes in the closet/bathroom/laundry room.
    Reaching out more.
    Eating strange combinations of things.
    Hiding from the teacher during virtual yoga class.
Go easy. Chin up.

This is not an interruption. It's a rupture. We are going to live in a different world on the other side of this. There's a lot outside our control right this minute, but we get to decide what that world looks like. I'm in for that. Chin up.

The "I love when you start things with 'I have a crazy idea'" friend is a very special kind of person. Here's to people who are willing to go out on a limb with us. Chin up.

When I remember to embrace my inner [...], and bring it out to meet the world (metaphorically) (for now), I am usually pleasantly surprised. Let us not hide our fun bits! Chin up.

This tree.
This morning.
The quiet.
This cup of tea.
The first check-in.
This moment.
This month
(or maybe the next)
(or the one after that).
Chin up.

Historically, March has not been my month. It's like every year's March tries to outdo the previous March in terribleness. And then March 2020 came along and laughed in the face of all other Marches. Anyway, we have a long road ahead, but April, I'm glad you're here. Chin up.

It seems to me that we talk about the before and the after. Maybe that's why I constantly forget that the in-between is where all the messy stuff is. 2020 is shaping up to be a year of in-between. (Let's not waste it.) Chin up.

Look for the helpers, Mr. Rogers said, and that's solid advice. Look also for the people who need us. Look for the meaning, and accept the not-knowing. Look for the strength, look for the softness, remember that we may find them together. Look to ourselves. Again, again. Chin up.

> Good morning! A new day. A new chapter. A new chance. Begin it. Chin up.

April 4, 2020

I am astounded by the many different ways in which people extend grace and care. It's confirming and necessary and warm when our ways match up; it's provoking and bright and magical when they diverge. Keep extending, however you do it. Chin up.

When we're on the other side of this: What will we have taken with us? What will we have left behind? What will we change because of right now? It seems worth aiming for perspective, after all. Chin up.

If ever there was a time to dig into the complexity of something, this would seem to be it. When it comes to things that matter, skimming the surface doesn't serve us well. We've got to dive deep. Chin up.

Truth and wisdom are all around. Always, always, even in the midst of a lot of muck, there is at least one kernel I need to hear. Why do I continue to be surprised by that? Chin up.

April 8, 2020

I may be wearing sweatpants, but (and!) THERE WILL BE NO SMALL ACCOMPLISHMENTS TODAY. (Some days we must hold ourselves upright by sheer force of wildly optimistic will.) Chin up.

2020 is a year of vulnerability, individual and collective. A year of "this is not at all how I thought it would go." A year of change. Of mourning. Of discovering who our people are. 2020 is a year of falling apart and, if we make it so, the start of coming together. Chin up.

This morning, I laid in bed and mentally categorized my sweatpants. Happy Saturday, friends. Chin up.

The blossoms are showing off for us this year. (Or maybe I'm just noticing them more?) I like to think that the earth is whispering to us, "still here, hold on." Chin up.

Chin up (even when you (hypothetically) fall flat on your face and scrape said chin).

You know what really gets me jazzed up? The things that people are excited about. All of you with your hobbies and interests and talents and affinities and collections make me happy. Enthusiasm is the first thing, the biggest thing. Bring it! Chin up.

"I'm not coping well right now" is something I announced loudly this morning. As if voicing it at volume would relieve some of the anger and sadness and fear and restlessness and frustration. Some days the best we can do is say our feelings out loud. Chin up.

> Being brave does not require feeling brave. (Sometimes I forget that.) Chin up.
>
> *April 16, 2020*

2020 is the year of the virus and isolation and struggle and loss. But it's also the year of the mask crafters, the letter writers, the t-shirt makers, the birds outside my window, those who share poetry, the bread bakers, the bell ringers. Keepers of community, all. Chin up.

Time has entered its own loop, detached from our existence. I don't think we can trust it anymore, friends. Yes, it's hokey but I'll say it anyway: The thing we can rely on is each other. Physically distanced, connected in community. Love is our loop. Chin up.

Confession: A friend helped me realize that I am smiling less at strangers because I feel silly smiling while wearing a mask. Being self-conscious is the silly thing because WE NEED *ALL* OF THE KIND EYES RIGHT NOW. (I'm practicing by smiling at all of you.) Chin up.

Today: just one small thing. One tiny step forward. One circle of ground held. One inquiry. One piece of clarity. One paragraph. One bell rung. One real conversation. (Then, when we're ready, the next.) Chin up.

I don't know about you, but in this time I've learned some things about myself that I'd like to unlearn. Such as: I will eat frosting out of the can given the opportunity. Also, I apparently say *all* of my feelings out loud. A little self-knowledge goes a long way. Chin up.

I try to remind myself: Every day feels the same, but the truth is that nothing is static. The world is changing by the minute, and so are we. Now is not always. Chin up.

Words with intent can change us. Some people just make us smarter, sharper, funnier, braver, prettier. May your day include at least three of those people! (More would be good.) Chin up.

The thing about letting go is not that emptiness rushes in, but that it settles, still and opaque. We have to do all the hard things: sit with it, get comfortable with its silence, wait. Eventually, we will have changed enough that we can begin to see what's underneath. Chin up.

Grateful and resentful. Restless at home and anxious outside. Reaching out to people because connection and pushing away because so much talking. Heart filled and heart breaking. Life is paradox, especially now. Chin up.

Care doesn't sound like much, but it's a fierce concept. "To attach importance." Caring is earnest and fumbling. It means being vulnerable. We each have our own care language; it can come out in lots of ways, and some of them are nuanced. May we care boldly! Chin up.

For those of us who think we can see around all corners, it can be hard to let go of negative input. But it's okay to lean towards the things that give us energy and make us feel strong. Don't give space to anything that drags us down, not today. Chin up.

Our lives work in strange ways. Sometimes one thing turns into a whole bunch of other things, and we have to pursue each and every one because: life. We might end up back where we started, or we might forget where (or why) we started. Let's not squander the meandering. Chin up.

There are times when you just don't want to be encouraged. Some days, you want to lay your head down, take a few minutes (or hours) of feeling sorry or sad or scared, and maybe cry it all out loud. That's okay, for sure. The rest of us will keep lookout. Chins up, team.

> Keep track of the people who believe in you. I'm serious. Make a list. Do it right now. Marvel at the people on your team. Thank the universe for its generosity and brilliance. The time is coming (perhaps it's now?) when you'll want to call out each one by name. Chin up.

April 30, 2020

Sometimes trying looks like flailing. Sometimes resting looks like doing nothing. Sometimes caring looks like worrying. Sometimes doing one thing looks like avoiding another. None of that matters; who cares what it looks like? We get you. Chin up.

These days, there's a lot of adjusting, and then readjusting, and then adjusting again. And worrying about the adjusting. And overthinking the adjusting. And pre-gaming the adjusting that is to come. It turns out we're way more flexible than we thought. (Multitudes!) Chin up.

I watched a video about the murder hornets yesterday. I'm pretty sure these giant agents of relentless mayhem and predation were sent as metaphor. We need to get the point, already. Pay attention. Reset the juju. Save the bees. Eyes open, chin up.

Fill in the blank: Now more than ever, the world needs more [ ]. Okay. Bring all you have, and let's go make a world of [ ] real. Chin up.

When I feel stuck, it often helps to make a list of my options. Sure, I might not like most of them, but there are almost always more options than I expect. Or if there aren't, there's the reality of seeing that. (Sign up for my "list-making as life management" course.) Chin up.

Yesterday someone asked me, what are you waiting for? And that, my friend, is when I remembered that sometimes the right question shows up in your life at exactly the right time. Chin up.

People look different in light and shadow, a wise person told me. Heck yes, I thought. Life has shown that to be true. And then like all good pieces of wisdom, it whispered, this also applies to you. And, well, yes. Chin up.

Write a letter. Bake a cake. Sing a song. Design the emoji you've been waiting for. Make a paper chain. Doodle on a post-it. Dance on your BFF's lawn. I don't much have an opinion on what it is but would you put something positive into the world today? (Thank you.) Chin up.

Because timing is a very real thing, and so is readiness, for today, I'm not going to ask the questions for which it's too soon to know the answers. Chin up.

Time and blooming trees and noisy birds and my beloved places and most of all my people. My best offer is imperfect love, my heart breaking and swelling. Chin up, my friends.

So there's been some spontaneous and surprise emotions lately. But also, the hummingbirds are back, and there are hot pink blossoms on the tree in front of the building next door, and sunset is 7:55 p.m. Chin up.

When you ask, "what do you see that I don't/can't/won't?," people will blow you away with their responses. Also, my people are brilliant and creative and insightful and generous. Lots of light, through them. Chin up.

My default is to focus on negative feedback. Right now, it's okay to say a polite but cool thank you to anything that is wrapped in criticism and turn away. Yes, feedback is a gift, but we are doing imperfect, weighty, magical human work every day. (Most days, at least.) Chin up.

It's nice to have people who believe in you. And by nice I mean exhilarating, humbling, and terrifying (but in the best kind of way). May we all believe, may we be believed in, may we rise to the belief. Chin up.

It turns out that I miss people. So I'm going to need you all to send me real, genuine smiles today. The kind that crinkle your eyes, please. Acceptable formats include photos, zoom, facetime, and standing outside my window. Chin up, to us all.

I've long wondered where my circle is. Yesterday, I realized: they're everywhere. Thoughtful, kind, vulnerable people are my jam. (I'm aspiring.) I see you all. Chin up.

Maybe a valuable thing is for each of us to nurture our ability to hold multiple competing thoughts at the same time. To admit the validity of two divergent truths. To contain paradox, to know it exists in ourselves and the world, to allow it to soften and strengthen us. Chin up.

Sometimes I need to remind myself that things are not always what they seem. Which is actually a plus, because the less obvious things are more fun. Chin up.

> Speak generously. Speak gently. Speak your wishes into admission into very existence. Speak healing. Speak struggle. Speak love to fear, to anger, to grief. Speak what needs to be said, what can only be said by you, with your words and actions and whole lives. Chin up.

I thought I had experienced most of the human feelings, but 2020 is feelings in technicolor. It is feelings animated. 3D feelings. Feelings in surround sound. All of the feelings sitting in my living room, waiting impatiently for family dinner. You know what that means. Chin up.

If we can screw up the courage to say the scary thing aloud, learn in public, risk being seen (or not seen), we will (at least 10% of the time) be richly rewarded by the receptivity of others. It's as though they were just waiting for us. (Good enough odds to try it.) Chin up.

May 21, 2020

The world sounds different this spring, doesn't it? I'm trying to listen better. Listen to my heart. Listen to my gut. To my mom. To the people who show up. My body. The music. Listen to the birds and trees, to the silence. So many glorious, confusing things to take in! Chin up.

There are times to back away from fear and times to move into it. Struggles that are meant to be worked through and those that are unwinnable by sweat or will. Truths that need to be heard and things that shouldn't be said. Seems to me, discernment is the biggest thing. Chin up.

A morning assessment. More: patience, humility, creativity, vegetables, focus. Less: snacking, sitting, procrastinating, swearing. Just right: Morning tweets, Springsteen listening, mixing my nouns and verbs and being totally okay with it. Chin up.

It's okay, some days, to have nothing to say. Chin up.

My world has shrunk a bit lately. I'm okay with it being just small enough for me to get my arms around, for me to carry inside my heart. (Could do with more hugs.) Chin up.

Isn't it amazing that in the same day someone can ask me the very question I most don't want to answer and two hours later someone else can say exactly the thing I didn't know I needed to hear? I'm over here just reeling from the wisdom of the universe. Chin up.

My life is infinitely better when I fill my heart with people who do hard things, create beauty, care a lot, say wow a lot, smile generously, risk looking ridiculous, and try to put words to the moment. (Luckily, when I look for them, they're everywhere.) Chin up.

May 28, 2020

Sometimes, when we have an idea, we just have to run with it. Sure, it might be a terrible mistake that will haunt us (chances are slim), but the enthusiasm, the risk, the possibility are worth it. Go forth, try. Chin up.

To paraphrase someone smart: we've got to get the question right. There are big and little questions, and sometimes it's confusing which is which. Sometimes we have to answer the now questions before we can get to the next question. Point is, what are we asking? Chin up.

Listen up. Show up. Speak up. Hearts out. Chin up.

The world is different when we allow ourselves to see more fully the things before us. We are different when we allow ourselves to feel more fully the things we carry with us. Chin up.

Today. Chin up.

The Gates of Hope
Victoria Safford

*Our mission is to plant ourselves at the gates of Hope—
Not the prudent gates of Optimism,
Which are somewhat narrower.
Not the stalwart, boring gates of Common Sense;
Nor the strident gates of Self-Righteousness,
Which creak on shrill and angry hinges
(People cannot hear us there; they cannot pass through)
Nor the cheerful, flimsy garden gate of
"Everything is gonna' be all right."
But a different, sometimes lonely place,
The place of truth-telling,
About your own soul first of all and its condition.
The place of resistance and defiance,
The piece of ground from which you see the world
Both as it is and as it could be
As it will be;
The place from which you glimpse not only struggle,
But the joy of the struggle.
And we stand there, beckoning and calling,
Telling people what we are seeing
Asking people what they see.*

I'm pretty sure Neil Diamond was on to something when he told us to turn on our heartlight. Make it glow. Chin up.

The tiny speck of possibility that kindles warmth and brightness in your soul? Notice it. Speak kindly to it. Spark it. Chin up.

Outrage and tenderness. Accountability and possibility. Past and future. Unrelenting heartache and tiny moments of joy. Our bravest humans are holding all of us in the balance. Chin up.

There are times when I let being shy get in the way of being truly, deeply, personally, meaningfully kind. Of holding a connection. Of receiving what has been offered. I need to stop doing that. Chin up.

One short moment of internal quiet. Clarity (or at least patience for the lack of clarity), a purpose and a team, grace for my mistakes. Room to move. A sign from the universe (as obvious as possible, please). Chin up.

Have we all decided who we want to be today? There won't be much time once the day gets going, and it's better to decide ahead so we don't have to think about it in the moment. Chin up.

Sometimes I might need the tough love approach, but let's just say, it's not my favorite. As a general rule, it doesn't hurt to save that for a backup plan. Chin up.

It isn't easy business, holding up our end of humanity. Take good care of your hearts, take good care of each other, hold steady. Chin up.

Life brings us into contact with people and places and ideas that touch our souls. May we welcome them, even when it hurts (so good). We are ever remaking ourselves. Chin up.

Certain things are better when embraced without restraint. For me, these things include enthusiasm, kindness, ice cream cake, curiosity, little free libraries, and balloons. Go unabashedly, unashamedly, irrepressibly, unequivocally all in, on something. Chin up.

There are lots of unpleasant things we have to put up with in life, like vegetables and dental floss and alarm clocks. So let's completely avoid the terrible, unnecessary things. Like small talk, low-fat cheese (low-fat anything), bad books, and uncomfortable shoes. Chin up.

I've been thinking a lot about how we carry the load together, over the long term. Who can I spell, how can I support? It matters how we show up in service of each other in this world. Chin up.

This morning, when I went inside myself for something to say to you, there's only blank space. Maybe you need quiet, too, or maybe you will fill the silence with what needs to be said. Chin up.

The gaps between: Who we are and what we feel. What we do and what we *could* do. Me and you. My heart and my head. Intention and impact, process and outcome. Then and now. What was said and what was heard. There's a lot more space than I often remember. Chin up.

> There is extraordinariness all around. If we're doing it right, we fall at least a tiny bit in love with all of it. Chin up.

June 17, 2020

Whatever we've locked away in our vaults because it makes us feel a little uneasy or unsettled (or too powerful), today is a good day to take it out. Try it on. Preen, if appropriate. (We can always put it back.) (Or not.) Chin up.

Thinking a lot about fault lines—geological, emotional, social, generational, spiritual. Unimaginable new conditions are created when things endlessly bump up against each other. Let us be transformed. (No going back.) Chin up.

Reminder to myself: Selfishness is not always active consumption. Sometimes it's the passivity of looking away from a truth, refusing to hear, forgetting, doing nothing. Stop doing that. Chin up.

Fire in your belly. Light in your soul. Sparkles before your eyes. Sunlight through your window. Chin up. 🔥

I can hear something 10 times, 1,000 times, and not absorb it. But every once in awhile it pops up right at the moment I need it, like magic. Our minds are funny. Chin up.

Some people glow like candlelight. Some glow like sunrise. Some burn like fire. Some people shine bright and fast and sudden like motion-activated porchlights. Some sparkle like a thousand flashbulbs. Some beam steady like a lighthouse. There's light within us all. Chin up.

There is shadow as well as light within each of us. And that's okay. Don't be afraid to nose around in the dark places, you might find something good. (You might find something we've been looking for.) Chin up.

June 24, 2020

Let's tell the truth. The good, the bad, the ugly. The proud and painful, the embarrassing and excruciating, the tender, the complicated. Let's have faith in our ability to hear it, hold it. Let's start there. Chin up.

Internal debate: Is purpose something to chase after or wait for it to land upon us? (Alternating abruptly between the two doesn't seem to be a great option.) (Oh, maybe that's the point.) Chin up.

> Look at all the loveliness and possibility and charm and care-taking and strength and humor and wisdom and making-something-beautiful-where-there-was-nothing all around us. Marvel! Chin up.

A working theory: The better the questions, the less the answers matter. Chin up.

Love your people with all the madness and softness and restlessness and sweetness and ridiculousness and wholeness in your soul. All of it. Chin up.

I am fairly certain that becoming a real, grown up, three dimensional person has something to do with learning how to gracefully accept when options become impossibilities. (Still working on this.) Chin up.

Life requires a lot of bending. Sometimes we get all wonderfully stretchy. Sometimes something important snaps. Challenge is, we don't always know which will happen, and we don't always get to say when. Chin up.

Tell me who you have faith in. What you think about when you wake up in the middle of the night. The price you'd pay for that thing. (Yes, that one.) Tell me why you're on fire. What you would give voice to, if there were just one more sentence left to say. (Say it.) Chin up.

July 2, 2020

I have a jar of beach rocks, my grandmother's eyes, stubborn restlessness, a copy of Little Women I got for $4.95 at Job Lot 30 years ago, my dad's definitions of hard work and good bread, and a lot of pens. Every ancestor. Every choice. What do you carry with you? Chin up.

How might we (I) make this year, place, world (me) a tiny bit more bearable? Chin up.

I am always rewarded when I choose to: Take joy in others' accomplishments. Replace defensiveness with curiosity. Put down the uninteresting book. Pause before responding. Pause before the second (third) cookie. Smile. Here's to good choices. Chin up.

Hold on to the people who see you, who think you're funny, who get the way you view the world, who smile when you smile, who hear when you say something important, who take a tiny bit of your being into their hearts. Those are your people; they are rare and precious. Chin up.

Why do I forget that the path connecting idea to plan to implementation to results is long, meandering, and unseeable? The good and bad news is that there's lots of room for things to happen along the way. Stay alert. Settle in. Chin up.

Lesson of the morning: It is always good to say thank you, even when it feels awkward and comes out weird. Gratitude > embarrassment. Chin up.

> For good and bad, threshold moments are when we are most human. We remember our arrivals and departures. We remember how we felt when we had to say something that was difficult and necessary. Don't let thresholds pass unnoticed, for you or your people. Show up extra. Chin up.

Whatever light and magic there will be in the next few moments, it's going to come from within us. No pressure, but dig deep. Chin up.

We gather our people, our snacks, our Saturday pants, words that bring us meaning, our fight songs and theme songs, our comfort items...all for company as we go. And at the end of the day, it comes down to just what's inside of us. Absorb what we can. Chin up.

"Strong at the broken places" is one of life's great ironies. Also: Bravery through vulnerability. Things that taste so good being so bad for you. Learning way more through failure than success. Life is really ironic, it turns out. Chin up.

Make room. For other people, for what is necessary, for what is good, for reactions (the universe's and your own), for what is coming. Chin up.

Sometimes the universe allows us temporary glimpses into alternative realities, as if we had chosen different adventures. We can't stay in what might've been, but we can peek in for a few minutes. (That may be long enough.) Chin up.

The beginning and the end get most of our attention (and for sure, it helps to get those right) (whatever that means), but it seems to me that a lot happens in the middle. (The messy, murky, is it even making sense? middle.) Keep pulling that thread. Chin up.

Reminder to self: There is no all-this-way or none-that-way. Stop looking for easy answers through absolutes, stop soothing confusion by drawing false boundaries. Open to nuance and complexity, accept that some understandings take a long time. Seek people who do that. Chin up.

There are people who sparkle. Admit it. When you see them or think about them, they are framed by sparkles. My sparkly people and your sparkly people may be different, which is great because it means everyone sparkles for someone. Chin up.

Make some good trouble today and tomorrow. Do it because we can, because we should. Do it for John Lewis, for everyone who has fought valiantly the fights that need fighting. Stand tall on the shoulders of heroes. Chin up.

I read somewhere/sometime that it takes two months to form a habit. I'm pretty sure that must be an average, because good habits take me like 1,543 days and bad habits require just one occurrence to be stuck for life. (Bring on the post-breakfast hostess cupcake!) Chin up.

There are moments to rise to, moments to live through, moments to live for, moments to live in, moments to make meaning of, moments to meet. Which is this? Chin up.

If I can't stop myself from asking the insufferable question (is this what there is?) I can learn to give a better answer (yes, and isn't it glorious?). Chin up.

Is an idea any good if it doesn't go through a *what the holy heck was I thinking?* phase? Chin up.

I asked friends to help me commemorate my 40th birthday by sharing their own Chin Up messages. Here are some favorites.

BIL HERRON: Hey, thoughtful and caring people out there: I get that the noise and vitriol and performative yelling we're surrounded by makes you want to retreat into your shell. But that's why we need your presence, your voice, your fortitude. Showing up beats showing off. Chin up!

MATTHEW BILLINGS: "Don't bend; don't water it down; don't try to make it logical; don't edit your own soul according to the fashion. Rather, follow your most intense obsessions mercilessly." Kafka. "Mercilessly"—chin way up!

BRENT RUNYON: Some days it's just too hard to get up and go for a run. There are other days. Have a muffin. Chin up.

RAMAN SHAH: To be childlike enough to imagine the world can be good—but mature enough to grind through the hard parts and slow parts—is where the action is. #chinup

JOCK HAYES: HOPE is a bargain we make with ourselves—buoyed by faith in any number of things (rituals, spirits, charms and mysteries)—we lean into HOPE when we need it most & lean on it always. The power of persistent optimism often sheds light where there is little. #chinup

DEB BAUM: Chin up, the world need to see your smile.

KATHRYN CANTWELL: Our bodies and earth were naturally built to heal, #chinup

Mary-Kim Arnold: Happy 40th @JDinRI! you asked me if it gets better, and i think it does but of course it's complicated. my 40s have had moments of unexpected joy and heartbreaking devastation (and lots in between) i've been grateful for good company. welcome!

Gonzalo Cuervo: In these times, where everything seems possible and nothing seems real, there's a lot to learn from thoughtful, caring and present people like @JDinRI. #Chinup

Sue AnderBois: We just discovered our dog is afraid of flies. He's otherwise very rough and tumble. It made me think that sometimes you can run with dogs 3x your size. Sometimes you're afraid of houseflies & need a friend to hug you. You're still perfect. Chin up.

Angel Taveras: Wishing @JDinRI a happy 40th and doing my best #chinup as requested! Rev. Dr. Martin Luther King Jr.: "Our lives begin to end the day we become silent about things that matter..." Keep marching and making your voices heard! Chin up!

Toby Shepherd: "The reasonable man adapts himself to the world: the unreasonable one persists in trying to adapt the world to himself. Therefore all progress depends on the unreasonable man." Keep it unreasonable, @JDinRI—we depend on it! #ChinUp

Lois Kelly: Losing my fight to control the yellow jackets and poison ivy in my yard. But found homemade Toll House cookies in the freezer this morning. #chinup

Something I know: True fortune is people who have my back, whose hearts can hold me up, whose hearts can carry the whole world. Don't underestimate love. Chin up.

Knowing which things to do the same and how to make tweaks and when to blow it all up and start over, there's some real wisdom in that. Chin up.

Being polite is a thing. I'm not saying above all else or when unmerited or some arbitrary definition of etiquette. But on the whole, manners are a good starting place. Chin up.

Confident, yes; arrogant no. Accountability, yes; shame, no. Kind, yes; pushover, no. Determined, yes; obsessed, no. Strong, yes; rigid, no. Solitude, yes; lonely, no. Every good and useful thing has a shadow. Chin up.

Something I forget too often: When we try to hide our selfishness by wrapping it in pretend kindness, other people can always tell. Chin up.

> I must periodically remind myself: The fact that it is almost always easier to keep everything the same is not a good enough reason not to change. Chin up.

Saying something does not make it so. (Yes, the irony, I see it.) Chin up.

I heard someone define courage as "rage of the heart." I'm not clear on the etymology, but the point is: may we all live in such ways that, when we leave, a little bit of our heart rage stays behind. Chin up.

I hit a wall yesterday because of cruel policies, comparisons, questioning everything, too much time, not enough time, rudeness, sugar, things being broken, a splinter, motorcycle noises, and my own ridiculousness. But it's a new day (a new month), and we're back at it, chin up!

What lights you up? We each have our hills to charge, windmills to tilt at, fires to stoke. We are all curious, weary, valiant heroes along our very own journeys. Fight onward. Chin up.

Feedback is a gift.
Feedback is a gift.
Feedback is a gift.
Chin up.

At times, I'm confronted
by the many ways in
which I fail to show up as
I should, fail to do all I
can. This is scary and
embarrassing and
necessary. All of this to
say: I'm sorry, I will try
again, let's not give up on
me. Chin up.

Find one good thing. Linger over it, breathe, say thank you. Let that be our toehold for today. Maybe tomorrow there will be another. Chin up.

We're still in the messy middle, and we're going to be here awhile. Nothing clever to say today. Keep going. Just keep going. Whatever that means, however that looks. Our hearts are big enough for this. Chin up.

Once set into motion, some things have to happen. No amount of avoiding, strategizing, charming, or ignoring will prevent them. If we give up our illusions of control and let them happen, whatever is next can happen. Chin up.

Let's choose to see in each other first and most the good things—the strong and funny and brilliant and beautiful. Keep the best parts front and center; the rest can fill in around the edges. Chin up.

Expecting perfection (from ourselves, each other) is not reasonable (I'm told). Expecting humility, honesty, presence, though, that seems like tablestakes. Chin up.

To persist in some difficult thing that is meaningful and known only to you, there's glory in that. We all have our own mountains to climb. Chin up.

We remain connected with everything we have touched. Every person, every place stays inside of us, knotted together with every other. Sometimes we forget until life tugs on a thread in joy or sorrow. And then we remember. Chin up.

Telling myself: Do what is necessary. Do what is unnecessary for you but still needed by someone. Do what you say you will. Do more than that. Do something that brings light. Do something that brings delight. (Do something.) Chin up.

Sometimes the small choices have long tails. I wonder, what if we chose [...] instead of [...]? Some choices are past, of course, but some are right now. Chin up.

Watch your elbows, people. The world is treacherous enough right now, let's not cause any unnecessary damage. Chin up.

We assume that happy should be shared and sad must be experienced alone, and I'm not sure why. Share the struggle. There are those who will stand with us. Chin up.

There is both bitter and sweet as we approach the end of something important. Things to hold on to, things to let go of, ways to move on. Chin up.

Whatever you have today, give it to the world. All of it. (And take whatever you need.) Chin up.

Life is not performance art. Neither is relationship or community or humility or hard work. Pay attention to what it is, not what it looks like. Things that matter have substance, depth, messiness, shadows. Grind away, eyes on the horizon. Chin up.

Perhaps it comes down to this: Don't look away. No matter what, don't look away. Bearing witness is our sacred human duty. Chin up.

August 19, 2020

www.ingramcontent.com/pod-product-compliance
Lightning Source LLC
Chambersburg PA
CBHW041353290426
44108CB00006B/135